How Good Is *The Givers and The Takers?*

"A magical, life-changing book! A must-read for Givers. Takers will avoid it...but that's okay."

—BARBARA STANNY
Prince Charming Isn't Coming: How Women Get Smart about Money

"Being a Giver is no better or worse, healthy or less healthy, than being a Taker. This book will help you recognize the manipulative potential in both personalities."

—*THE SAN FRANCISCO EXAMINER*

"A valuable, much-needed book. A vivid portrayal of the two types of people."

—MARY EARLE CHASE, author of *Waiting for Baby*

"A fine read—swift, pointed and practical. An operator's manual for dealing with Givers and Takers."

—CANDICE FUHRMAN, author of *Publicity Stunt*

"A true original! Everything you need to know about Givers and Takers—their posture, friendships, temperament amd desires. Compelling!"

—KATHRYN DELONG, editor

"Superbly crafted and astonishingly powerful! A wonderful guide that presents a clear description of Givers and Takers as polar opposites. A transforming book."

ART BROWNSTEIN, M.D., *Healing Back Pain Naturally*

"Givers and Takers simplified! A treasure."

JANET LUHRS, *Simple Loving* and *The Simple Living Guide*

Also by Bruce Feld

Cleopatra in the Night
The Significance of Love, Etc.
Listen to the Duchess
Whiskey and Wheaties
Love Children

Also by Cris Evatt

How to Organize Your Closet...and Your Life!
How to Pack Your Suitcase...and Other Travel Tips
Opposite Sides of the Bed
Simply Organized!
30 Days to a Simpler Life

The
Givers
-and the-
Takers

Cris Evatt & Bruce Feld

PAPAYA PRESS
KAUAI, HAWAII

For Lucy, Theo and Dave

PAPAYA PRESS
P. O. BOX 223157
PRINCEVILLE, HI 96722

Copyright © 1983 by Crislynne Evatt and Bruce Feld

Specified excerpts from THE MOVIE QUOTE BOOK
by Harry Haun (Lippincott & Crowell, Publishers)
Copyright © 1980 by Harry Haun. Reprinted by permission of
Harper & Row, Publishers, Inc.

Book and Cover Design: Melissa Cohen

Originally published by Macmillan Publishing, Co., 1983.
Ballantine Books Edition, May 1988.

Library of Congress Catalog Card Number 82-21705

ISBN 0-9708181-0-6

Psychology/Self-Help

First Papaya Press Edition: 2002

10 9 8 7 6 5 4 3 2 1

Printed in the United States by
Morris Publishing
3212 E. Hwy 30 • Kearney, NE 68847
1-800-650-7888

Contents

Foreword.....7

Before You Begin....9

1. "But, I Do Both!".....11

2. Thirty Giver-Taker Traits.....25

3. Who Chases Whom?.....63

4. The Taker's Secret Code.....71

5. The Lovers' Triangle.....79

6. Rating the Two Types.....85

7. The Remedies.....93

Foreword

We are all born into an age of remarkable complexity. Some of this complexity has arisen from the rapid explosion of electrical, chemical, and mechanical technology; some from the internal journeys of scientific and humanistic psychology. The growing world of words and concepts in psychology is perhaps more confusing because of the multiple sources of wisdom. These sources run the gamut from popular news columns that dispense psychotherapy on the prompting of a sentence or two of data, to technical articles that statistically analyze smaller and smaller increments of minutia.

Amid this morass of psychological ideas, Feld and Evatt have introduced an elegant and yet simple construction, "Givers and Takers," with which they piece together the puzzle of everyday psychological experience. The words are not new. The idea itself in not new, being firmly rooted in the most academic and traditional of psychological theories.

What is new is that this secret—the fact that the world can be carved up so neatly—is finally out of the back rooms of psychotherapy offices and available to the general public.

Besides explaining interpersonal and emotional aspects of our world, Feld and Evatt have succeeded in triggering the "Which am I?"/"Who am I?"/"What am I?" response in the reader that is so essential to understanding the self.

The fact that the authors' division of the psychological world seems simplistic should not stop you from appreciating the hidden depth in the concept. We must remember that one of the most complex devices of our time, the computer, is little more than an array of switches which turn either on or off. It is no insult for a man or woman to acknowledge that he or she has a very real simplicity lurking behind a mask of subtlety. The discovery of this simplicity is essential if we wish to act rationally in an ofttimes irrational world.

Rex Julian Beaber, PhD
Director of Psychological Services
UCLA Hospitals and Clinics

Before You Begin

Each of us was born a Giver or a Taker. We either over-give or over-take in our relationships with others. Fortunately, there are ways of modifying our behavior, which we shall explore in this book. But first we will attempt to define the two basic personality types: the Giver (an outer-directed person) and the Taker (an inner-directed person). Each of us is predominantly one type of the other, not both. We may appear to be both types, so it is sometimes difficult to tell which we are. But it can be done.

Most of our knowledge about the two types of people is based on over one thousand personal interviews, our observations of couples interacting, and the results of our questionnaire. Our impetus to write this book came from the anguish we experienced in our own personal relationships. We continue, on a daily basis, to review couples and refine our conclusions. And the findings to date suggest that almost every couple consists of one Giver and one Taker—and that in the majority of these relationships there is an imbalance which places persistent stress on the both parties, often to the point where the relationship collapses.

Being a Giver is not superior to being a Taker. The reader is urged to discount the usual connotations of these terms. We might just have easily have called this book The

Winners and the Losers, in which case the disclaimer would have to be made that Winners are not superior to Losers.

Both Givers and Takers find themselves playing manipulative roles, which we shall discuss in detail. It is our hope that people who are caught in role-playing and are not aware of it will come to a greater understanding of the games they are playing. Whether or not they wish to continue playing games is their affair. Analysis—and our primary concern is to help the reader understand himself or herself to a greater degree—throws light on the furniture of the mind; it does not rearrange it. That rearranging is the individual's choice, the individual's responsibility, the individual's decision.

Cris Evatt and Bruce Feld

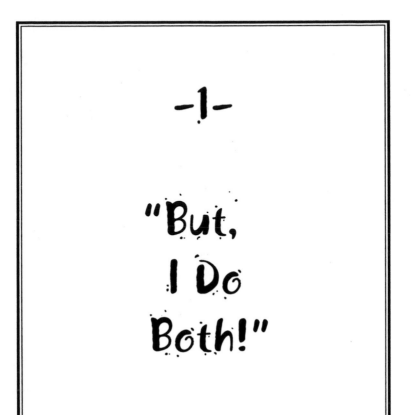

-1-

"But,
I Do
Both!"

*Most hit songs describe a Giver
crooning about a seductive Taker whom
he or she is chasing, losing, or winning.*

*True love has nothing to do with
the idolizing of one person by another.*

*In many love affairs, there is
one who loves and one who permits
himself to be loved.*

Whenever we tell someone that people are either Givers or Takers, we get this common response: "I do both!" That's because you do—but probably not equally. Almost everyone thinks his or her own romantic relationships exhibit an equal amount of giving and receiving by each party. "I wouldn't be in a relationship if things weren't pretty equal," is the belief. But haven't you heard the following comments about your friends?

About women friends: "Kimberly should watch out or she'll end up with another guy like her ex, Jason. He really used her!" Or, "Tara is so mean to her men. I can't believe they don't see through her."

About men friends: "Ryan is such a nice guy. Why doesn't he date women who appreciate him?" Or, "Alex is such a jerk! He goes out with other women and Justine puts up with his shenanigans."

The people described above are not rare. They are the same people who tell us they have equal relationships. That's because there is confusion as to what is giving and what is taking. After we define each type in the next chapter, you may be more reluctant to declare you are both.

In addition to the complaint that people are a mixture of both types, and you can't label them one or the other, there is another major objection: "Your Giver/Taker categorization is too black and white, too simplistic." Life is confusing and complex, we are told. Is it really?

☙ ☙ ☙

We believe there are tragic consequences to the fact that most lover relationships consist of one Taker and one Giver. The American painter James McNeill Whistler divided the world into patients and nurses. We believe that in many marriages one partner functions as the patient while the other functions as the nurse. Then, sadly, the patient becomes bored by the fact that he is constantly being served—and guilty over the fact that he does so little—while the nurse becomes resentful over the many unreciprocated chores she performs. In some marriages, of course, the wife is the patient and the husband the nurse.

What follows are ten lessons about Givers and Takers. We will begin by speaking generally, before discussing more concrete behavior in the following chapter, "Thirty Giver-

Taker Traits." It is the natural resistance of the mind to the simple notion of Givers and Takers that has kept the Giver/Taker Theory a secret for so many years.

LESSON 1
Giving and taking are flows of energy from one person to another.

The energy expended in a romantic relationship takes many forms. Some of it is physical and some emotional. Measuring it is not an easy task. It is because people have difficulty adding up what they have given and received that relationships become one-sided. We have found that the Giver expends a tremendous amount of energy for the benefit of his/her mate, while the Taker mate expends energy for himself/herself. Energy flows from the Giver toward the Taker.

LESSON 2
True reality can be divided into subjective and objective reality.

There are two realities—objective reality and subjective reality. Objective reality is the world beyond you. It is comprised of people, things, and events outside of you. Subjective reality is your inner world, your feelings and perspective. Your attention swings between the two.

Unfortunately, many of us enter this world with an

affliction. Our awareness of one of the realities is repressed—to some degree—and our awareness of the other is exaggerated. Consequently, we concentrate too exclusively on our inner world, or we concentrate too exclusively on our outer world, depending on whether we are Takers or Givers. We think we live equally in both worlds. Were this true, we would be Balanced. Sadly, this is not the case for most people.

Certainly, we talk about both worlds, but physically and emotionally we exist more in one than the other. For instance, people who never pamper themselves tell us about all the wonderful things they get in life, and then several days later complain about how little they have. Which is true? Our tendency to speak in opposites makes it difficult to know whether we are a Giver or a Taker.

LESSON 3
Givers have a stronger objective reality.
They are more other-focused.

People with a dominant objective reality put more energy into their outer world. They are more aware of others and less aware of themselves; consequently, they do more for others and less for themselves. That is why we call them Givers.

In a romantic relationship, a Giver focuses on the wants of his/her mates. Most Givers do about ten times more for their partners than their partners do in return. Givers get such joy from giving that most of the time they don't even notice that they do so much of it.

Givers communicate with their reality (the outer world) by pouring physical and emotional energy into it. One of the main ways Givers give is by talking. They use talk to cheer people up, solve others' problems, and make everything nice. The Giver may not realize how sensitive he is to the outside world. If someone lets a Giver know he is disliked, the Giver will be hurt, often to the point of being highly emotional and melodramatically defensive. Takers couldn't care less.

LESSON 4
Takers have a stronger subjective reality. They are more self-focused.

People with a dominant subjective reality put more energy into their inner world. They are more aware of themselves and less aware of others; consequently, they do more for themselves and less for others. That is why we call them Takers.

In a romantic relationship, Takers are very concerned with their wants, and so are attracted to mates who will put energy into satisfying them.

Takers encourage the flow of energy in their direction by constantly asking for things, and by charming or seducing people. Takers have as many subtle tactics for receiving as Givers have for giving.

For instance, Takers intimidate constantly, keeping Givers on the defensive. And when they do give, they unconsciously calculate the amount of energy required for the task. They allot a carefully measured (and always remembered) portion of giving. Givers, on the other hand, give automatically and constantly, hoping always to gain another's approval.

LESSON 5
Givers feel loved when they are giving, and Takers feel loved when they are receiving.

True love is unconditional giving and receiving. What Givers and Takers do is conditional. They expect the players in their drama to behave in a predictable way.

How Givers Love. Givers do not really love their mates; they love adoring and worshipping. They get excited by their mate's beauty or intelligence or charm. Givers want to serve, idolize, and possess someone they feel is attractive. Giving to such a person makes them feel loved. Givers experience infatuation; Takers do not.

How Takers Love. Takers do not really love their mates; they love being adored and worshipped. They get excited by the way that their mates express admiration for their beauty, intelligence, and charm. Takers want to be served, idolized, and possessed by someone they feel is worthy of them. They are bought in dozen of ways. Receiving from Givers makes them feel loved. Takers do not experience infatuation for others; they are already infatuated with themselves.

Real love is not a manipulation. Most hit songs describe a Giver crooning about a seductive Taker whom he or she is chasing, losing, or winning. True love has nothing to do with the idolizing of one person by another. It is based on mutual respect—not a master/slave interaction.

LESSON 6
Givers have trouble receiving and Takers have trouble giving.

How Givers Receive: Observe a Giver receiving from a Taker mate. She becomes touched, thrilled, occasionally blushes, and always feels honored. "Ah, he really does love me," she thinks fondly. These instances are rare in the life of the average Giver. On the other hand, true receiving is a constant activity, one that is acted out in many and varied ways.

If you have no trouble receiving from your mate, you have been getting enough and receiving is taken for granted. If you find yourself acting like the Giver mentioned above, then you are not receiving abundantly. You are thrilled with each gift because you receive so few.

How Takers Give: Takers hate to give because they usually have to make a conscious effort to do to, whereas Givers do it automatically. They always give in a showy way, bragging about their effort (which reveals how much they dislike the act). And Takers feel forced to obey their own code of reciprocation (i.e., "If someone gives me A, then I must give B.").

LESSON 7
Romantic relationships dramatically reveal Givers and Takers.

When you are in public, you are inhibited. You take on a courteous demeanor. Even the meanest people curb themselves around strangers. When you are with friends, you relax a little. When you are with your parents, you relax a lot. Yet the one who knows you best is your lover. It is primarily in a romantic relationship that you let the barriers fall.

Givers do many things with their lovers they would never do in public. They are more giving, more adoring, more easily hurt. They are also whiny and jealous. Givers are emotional people who act more emotionally in the presence of the their mates than with anyone else.

Takers are most themselves, too, when they are with their lovers. They can be more reserved, more charming, or more demanding. Takers express a hot-and-cold temperament at home, although on the job they control themselves...until perhaps they have reached a position of power.

People let it all hang out around their mates. It is in intimate relationships that you have the opportunity to see who you really are—a Giver or a Taker.

LESSON 8
Givers are sexually attracted to Takers, and vice versa.

Givers and Takers mate with each other by necessity. Givers are looking for someone to give to; Takers are looking for someone who will give to them. Of the hundreds of couples we have observed, the overwhelming preponderance have been couples consisting of one Giver and one Taker.

Givers thrive on adoring; Takers thrive on Giver energy. The subconscious urge to give or to be given to is one of the significant aspects of the mystery of love. Still, too often this union of opposite types results in misery. Opposites attract and attack.

You may be wondering, "Can Givers fall in love with Givers and Takers with Takers?"

Yes, but it happens rarely. When two Takers get together, we call it a Merger. In this case, the Takers are more interested in what they can offer each other—often financially. When two Givers get together, each may have been recently dumped by Takers. They get together to nurse each other's wounds.

LESSON 9
People who give too much harbor resentment, and people who take too much harbor guilt.

Givers feel displeasure because they grow to resent the imbalance of their Giver/Taker relationship. Even though Givers have trouble receiving, they still get upset or resentful when they realize, and they ultimately will, that they are not getting as much as they have given. Givers get tired of begging, pleading, and praying for favors from their mate.

Takers unconsciously suffer over the fact that they have taken too much from their lover. It may be a long time—if ever—before they acknowledge this guilt. *The Taker is as used to feeling guilty as the Giver is to being resentful.*

The downside of being a Taker is that she/he must put up with a mate who is sporadically quite bitter. In addition, the Giver is so predictable in giving that is becomes very dull to be around one. The Giver is like a dog you know will always wag his tail, even if you beat him occasionally. To the Taker, the Giver is mother and father, nurturer and nurse. The Giver, in short, is always there, loving you despite your flaws; boring you with consistency.

One woman asked us: "I give more to my mate than he gives to me, but I rarely feel resentful. Why is that?" Some Givers express their resentment loudly while others express it softly or not at all.

LESSON 10
It is not better to give than to receive; it is better to do both in equal portion.

We are brainwashed with the aphorism, "It is better to give than to receive." As an unfortunate result of this stance, Givers believe they are not giving enough and proceed to overexert. And Takers exploit this notion to the fullest, frequently whipping the Givers on to increase their output, most of which ends up conveniently in the Takers' laps.

Another aphorism which is similarly misleading goes, "If you give, it all comes back to you." Givers fall for this one, too; Takers do not. The statement is untrue. It ought to be read, "If you give to Givers, it all comes back to you; but if you give to Takers, you will get back about 10 percent."

The truth is, it is best to give and receive equally and abundantly, and if it's not happening make an adjustment. In romantic relationships, Givers ought to stand up to the Takers, and either receive what is their due or walk out. Likewise, Takers should abandon Givers who put out too much energy and are constantly resentful about it.

A truly Balanced Relationship has its own rewards. Takers who strive to give more will lose the burden of guilt that has weighed them down. Givers who take more will cease resenting others. And the difference in social relations will bring about a radically improved world.

Finally, for those Givers who feel smug about their constant charities to others, we urge this aphorism over all others: *"Physician, heal thyself."*

-2-

Thirty Giver-Taker Traits

*When Givers are with a suitor
who is very nice to them, they become
bored and disinterested.*

*And when Takers are with a suitor
who is very nice to them, they become
excited and interested.*

Giving and Taking are two "basic motives"
from which many behaviors spring.

This chapter concerns behavior in your most intimate relationships. You will be reading about many topics that are issues between you are your mate. Read about the two types of behavior then place a check or "x" in the box that describes your dominant behavior. *Both behaviors will describe you to some degree.*

Keep in mind that the thirty traits we describe may sound extreme in some instances. Also, you may have difficulty analyzing yourself. Naturally, it is tempting to choose the descriptions that suggest how you would like to be, not how you really are. This chapter is both a quiz and a reference section. You may use it after you have completed this book to quickly refer to the way the two distinct types act.

There is a tally sheet at the end of the traits. Transfer your markings from the definition pages to the tally sheet. Your answers will probably fall in both Giver and Takers sections. Few people are extreme Givers and Takers.

1. APOLOGIES

❐ Takers dodge apologies.

Takers do not understand why others view their actions unfavorably. "She's hurt over nothing. Why should I apologize?" he surmises. Rather than apologize, a Taker might say something like, "I want to be accepted for who I am." Comments like that attempt to make Givers feel guilty for expressing their point of view.

Takers tend to disrespect overly-apologetic people. Apologies are seen as powerless and self-deprecating. When Takers do apologize, their tone is less placating and more matter-of-fact than a Giver's. They like short apologies. Do apologetic people annoy you? Do you avoid apologizing whenever possible? If so, check the Taker box.

❐ Givers apologize readily.

Givers believe that apologies keep people on good terms with one another and build rapport. They look forward to opportunities to say, "I'm sorry," and cannot understand why anyone would refuse to apologize when it's so easy.

Givers apologize to keep the peace, which is more important for them than being right or top dog. Their tone is effusive and placating. They adore long, heart-felt apologies from others.

Do you apologize readily? Do you try to get others to apologize when you have been treated unfairly? And when you don't get an apology, do you say things like, "I deserve an apology from her." Or, "He refused to apologize to me." If so, check the box.

2. BREAKING UP

❐ Takers flee.

Takers usually leave Givers. Most often, but not always, this is the case. Why do Takers leave? They leave because they get bored. Imagine living with a Giver: The Giver is always amenable, always trying to please. Because of this the Taker feels the Giver is predictable, a follower—even though the Giver is often the louder, more talkative one who acts as if he/she is running the show. The Taker gets tired of having the real control.

The Taker also gets tired of the Giver's resentment and nagging. Givers have to expend more energy to be with a Taker, and often complain about it.

Are you usually the leaver? If so, check the box above?

❐ Givers hang on.

The Giver grieves, sheds tears, as the Taker makes an escape. "How could he/she leave me, after all I've done for him/her?" The Giver is perplexed. It is confusing to see someone go whom you have loved so passionately and devotedly. It takes months and sometimes years for a Giver to recover from the loss of a lover. "He/She was the love of my life, my soul mate." Takers dislike being labeled "soul mate," but go along with their Giver's story to keep them doting.

Breaking up becomes easier the more times you do it. It is a wise Giver who realizes that there is another Taker around the bend whom he/she can chase after.

In your relationships, are you frequently the one left behind, feeling ripped-off? If so, check the box.

3. CHANGING PEOPLE

☐ Takers seldom try to change others.

You can't change a Taker, so it's a waste of time to try. (Givers will at least try to change. They want to please.) And why should a Taker want to change? He/she likes the way he/she is. The Takers does what he wants to do, says what he feels, and has a supportive Giver for a mate. Life is good.

Takers rarely try to change their Giver mates. The Giver is there at their beck and call, willing to do almost anything they desire. Why tamper with a good thing? Also, it takes too much energy to change someone—and a Taker guards his energy tenaciously. For this reason, the Taker is not prone to giving advice, teaching, and correcting. "Leave people along and they'll figure it out" is his motto.

Who is described above—you or your lover? If it's you, check the box above.

☐ Givers frequently try to change others.

Givers want to change their Taker mates. They may think they are not attentive enough, are flirts, don't communicate, and are not very supportive. The list of desired changes is endless. The Giver is attracted to a self-absorbed type, and doesn't like it.

Givers reprimand themselves for wanting to change others. "I should accept him/her for the way he/she is—but I can't. I have standards."

Givers are good teachers. They enjoy telling people how to do things better, more efficiently—their way. They feel the urge to be motherly or fatherly.

Do you try to change people and then become frustrated when you don't get results? If so, check the box.

4. COMMUNICATION

☐ Takers are less verbal.

Takers talk far less than Givers do. And their conversation is of a different nature, too. Takers talk more about tangible matters. The men discuss their day at work, economic forecasts, football games, hiking trips, and their immediate plans. The women talk about their career, travel, design, and how well they are treated by the opposite sex. Givers, of course, discuss these things, too, but not as much; they prefer talking about peoples' problems, their feelings—deeper subjects.

Givers hurl questions at Takers to draw them out. Takers respond by squirming and retreating. The question "What are you thinking?" ruins their day. Are your the one who talks the least in your relationships? If so, check the box.

☐ Givers talk on and on.

Givers love to talk. They can go on and on about light matters or about their deep inner feelings. They'll tell you their whole life's history. Sometimes you wish they had an off-switch. Takers especially pray for this evolution because Givers can get very involved in telling how they feel, especially if they have been hurt.

Givers gossip more than Takers. The reason Takers gossip less is because they seldom think for long or deeply about other people. They would rather talk about "things" or "themselves." Givers use gossip to connect with one another. When they share gossip with Takers, they get the stink-eye.

In your relationships, do talk more than your mate? Voluminously. If so, mark the box here.

5. CONFLICT

☐ Takers are more confrontational.

At work, more Takers are apt to confront the boss than Givers. They tend to be competitive with anyone in authority. A Taker may feel better for having a fight and usually is able to "not take it personally."

In their romantic relationships, Takers often start a fight to release tension. One Taker male we know started a fight with his spouse because he didn't like the way she scooped ice cream "from the wrong end of the carton." Takers express their anger more directly than Givers and consider it a normal human emotion.

Are you more comfortable with conflict than your mate? If so, check the box in this section.

☐ Givers are less confrontational.

Generally speaking, Givers are intimidated by confrontation and don't see it as a game. (Many Takers relish power struggles.) Givers fear crossing the line. If they have a big fight at work, they think they will have to quit their job. Takers think they will have to have another fight.

In personal conflicts, Givers often feel hurt—not angry. "It upsets me when you....." The Taker then feels guilty and confused and says, "You're too thin-skinned. Lighten-up!" Also, Givers are quick to blame themselves for everything to diffuse a potential conflict.

If a Giver does starts a fights, it's usually over someone's bad behavior. "You shouldn't have done that..." Gr-r-r-r.

Generally speaking, are you the conflict-avoider in your relationships? Do you take things more personally than your mate does? If so, check the box above.

6. CONTROL

❏ Takers have more control.

Have you heard the story about the man who said, "I let my wife make all of the important decisions. I decide where we live, whom we visit, and where we go on our vacations. I let her decide whether we are in favor of a missile defense system." The man is obviously a Taker who controls the relationship.

Takers are quieter, more powerful people who exercise an authority that cannot be matched. It is a smart Taker who lets the Giver feel he/she has the power. Do you usually get your way on the issues that are the most important? If it's you, check the controller's box.

❏ Givers have less control.

Givers like what control they have and think they want more. They do not. They like being with a Taker who has strong opinions. It is one of the main reasons they are attracted to the Taker. They like a challenge, and Takers are stubborn and evasive.

Even though they are followers, Givers falsely view themselves as powerful because they talk more and act busier. The power of the Giver is illusory, not real. We have trouble convincing Givers of this. They don't realize that what power they possess is the power the Takers want them to have. Some very lazy ne'er-do-well Takers give all of the control to the Givers. These Givers are usually the loudest, happiest, and most aggressive of their kind.

Does your mate have the quiet power in your romantic relationship? If yes, then you are the Giver? Place a check in the box above.

7. DECISIVENESS

☐ Takers are more decisive.

Takers are more resolute. They firmly believe that "She who hesitates is lost." A Taker makes her decisions privately, and then checks them out with others, if she must. If a conclusion is not reached, then it's back to the drawing board.

Takers are often open to feedback after they have made a decision. They do not mind being challenged. Givers tend to think that Taker decisions are carved in stone because of their concise, forceful, self-directed deliveries. (And sometimes they are!)

Do you come to quick, strong conclusions that allow you to move forward? Do you make remarks like, "Let's get on with it!" And, "Don't go for perfection—go for completion." If so, check the box above.

☐ Givers are less decisive.

Givers hem and haw. They take more time with decisions because they take the human dimension more into consideration. Whether at work or at home, they want to figure out how a particular choice will affect others. Takers do this, too, but to a lesser degree.

Givers consult others more because they are more relationship-oriented. Consequently, they anguish over decisions after they have been made. They become concerned about what others may think.

Do you make a decision and then fret about its consequences? Do you say things like, "I hope my decision doesn't hurt her feelings." If so, check the box in this section.

8. ENGULFMENT

❒ A Taker's biggest fear is engulfment.

Takers have a compelling need for distance. They can only handle a certain amount of closeness—talking, pampering, affection, being together—and if that amount is exceeded, they pull away. However, most Takers don't know how to tell Givers they feel smothered and need space. So what do they do? They retreat—become silent, come home late, hide behind an Ayn Rand novel.

Sometimes Takers blame their mate for their feelings of engulfment—"You're smothering me!" Givers then feel confused, hurt, and unloved. In your relationships, are you usually the one who needs more space? If yes, mark the box above.

❒ A Giver's biggest fear is abandonment.

Givers are ineluctably drawn to people and tend to desire more closeness, connection, and intimacy. Even their posture leans toward others more than a Taker's. So what happens when a clingy Giver meets up with retreating Taker? The Giver feels abandoned—sad, lonely, anxious, desperate, and empty. Abandonment feelings are a natural outcome of making others one's primary focus.

Givers tend to blame themselves when their mate withdraws. "She must not love me. What am I doing wrong?" Rather than understanding that people have different needs for privacy and for connection, Givers often take retreating behaviors personally.

Do you experience feelings of abandonment more often than your mate does? If so, check the box above.

9. EXPECTATIONS

❏ Takers expect less of others.

Takers do not expect much more from their Giver than what they get, as long as they are being served and supported emotionally. Takers do not usually expect Givers to be more attractive or successful. They expect these things of themselves. If you had a gardener or a housekeeper, would you care if he or she is glamorous and ambitious?

Are you fairly comfortable with your mate as he or she is? Do you think that trying to change others is futile? If so, check the box above.

❏ Givers expect too much of others.

Givers want their mates to be worthy of all of the support and adoration they give them. If a Giver pays for schooling or helps start the fledgling business of a Taker mate, then he/she has expectations for the investment to pay off. Givers pressure Takers to live up to their fantasies. Unfortunately, the fantasy of the Giver is often higher than the Taker is capable of achieving.

Takers—the unsuccessful ones—feel they are bad investments, so often walk out on their relationships to the get the pressure off and assuage their guilt. Many Takers, of course, are independent financially and need Givers to support them in other ways.

Do you expect more than your mate is able or willing to deliver? Are you an interminable Hope Addict? Are you haunted by thoughts like, "I know he can do better." If yes, check the box above.

10. FACE VALUE

☐ Takers take words at face value.

Takers interpret words more literally than Givers do and are more matter-of-fact. They usually "say it like it is"— unless they are conning someone. Takers wonder why Givers go off on verbal tangents in search of hidden meanings.

Takers think, "Givers think about people too much. They are obsessed with the nature of relationships. Who cares why people do what they do?" To get along with Givers, Takers need to have patience with their need to analyze what others say and do.

Does your mate's propensity to come up with reasons for everything drive you crazy? Do you want to tell her: "Reasons are bullshit. Action is everything!"

Do you tend to accept things at face value and cast things as black or white? If this section resonates with you, check the box above.

☐ Givers search for hidden meanings.

Givers like to delve into the meaning of human actions. "Why does Ashley pick abusive men?" "What is the real reason why Brad left Daphne?" They casually ascribe people's behaviors to abusive childhoods or defective genes.

Givers are good at making gossip sound like psychoanalysis: "She acts weird because she comes from a dysfunctional family." Without them, the self-help section of bookstores would vanish. (We guesstimate that ninety-percent of our readers are Givers.)

Do you search for explanations for people's actions? Are you plagued by thoughts like, "There must be a reason why she....." If so, check the box above.

11. FEELINGS

☐ Takers talk less about their feelings.

"How do you feel about it, Reggie?" "Murmph!" Takers would rather act on their feelings than talk about them. They are calm and cool most of the time, and they suppress most of their emotions, except anger and rage.

Most Takers cannot handle an emotional outburst from a Giver that exceeds 10 minutes. If you are a Giver who tends to emote, carry a stopwatch—or be prepared to witness a Taker's hasty retreat.

Do you find it difficult, and unnecessary, to talk about your feelings? If your mate asks, "How do you feel?", do you freeze and think, "It's none of her business." Or do you tell her, "I'll be fine," when you're on the verge of a panic attack. If so, check the box above.

☐ Givers eagerly discuss their feelings.

Givers respond emotionally to many things that cause Takers to shrug and grunt. They openly communicate their fears and worries. Givers are not only better at expressing their feelings, but also at knowing the emotions of others.

A Taker is attracted to the Giver's emotional intensity. Her expressiveness makes him feel connected to her and very much alive. Later in the relationship, this attribute may be proof to him that she is irrational and unable to control herself.

Do you sometimes become frustrated because your mate is evasive? Are you tired of trying to guess what is going inside of his or her head? And do you share your feelings eagerly? If yes, check the box above.

12. FRIENDSHIPS

☐ Takers have fewer friends.

Takers can be loners more so than Givers. They feel more comfortable by themselves. The guy alone at the bar, observing others, is usually a Taker. Of course, there are Takers who are gregarious and loquacious. As a group, though, more Givers than Takers could be called glib, gabby, and gossipy.

Many Takers would rather do things with others—like hike, ski, attend a movie, or check out real estate—than just talk. They are highly action-oriented.

Interestingly, Takers have more platonic friends of the opposite sex than Givers do. They go to Givers for intimacy.

In your relationships, who usually has more friends—you or your mates? If it's you, check the box.

☐ Givers have more friends.

It is a rare Giver who does not have a flock of friends. Their phones are constantly ringing. Givers receive and send all kinds of cards and letters, and their Christmas list keeps growing.

Giver friendships tend to be more intimate, intense, and demonstrative than Taker friendships. Givers are easily affectionate to friends, and readily share personal thoughts and feelings that Takers tend to hold back. Oddly, Givers have fewer platonic friends of the same sex. They tend to be bored with opposites whom they find sexually unappealing.

If you tend to have more friends than your lover does, check the box above.

13. GIVING ORDERS

❑ Takers give orders bluntly.

Most Takers would rather give orders than receive them. To Takers, the person giving the orders is seen as superior and the receiver is seen as inferior. The Taker's world is dominated by ego, power, and competition.

To get someone to do something, you can appeal to them by commanding, demanding, requesting or suggesting...or nagging Takers prefer "commands" and "demands." Suggestions and requests are too soft and easy to dismiss, and nagging feels yukky.

Overall, do you feel more comfortable giving orders than your partner does? Do you dislike being ordered around by anyone, especially your mate—who you wish was respectful at all times? If this section hits home, check the box above.

❑ Givers give orders gingerly.

A Giver's orders often sound like suggestions and are prefaced with niceties like: "Would you mind if we...?" or "If it's not too much trouble, could you...?" Since Givers are highly concerned with the feelings of others, they are uncomfortable with giving direct orders that may offend the other person. Compliance, selflessness, and win-win strategies dominate the Giver's world.

Do you dislike issuing orders? Do you preface orders with compliments like, "I like the way you stack the firewood." Or phrase them as a question, "Could you wash the car on Sunday?" If this section rings true for you, check the box above.

14. INTIMIDATION

❐ Takers are more intimidating.

Most Takers do not know how good they are at getting others to do, or not do, something by inducing fear. Their silence can be daunting. Their direct, decisive mannerisms can be coercive. And their rage can be frightening. Takers, more than Givers, sneer, snarl, curse, and beat their chests to make a point.

In business, Takers use intimidation tactics to negotiate deals and move up the corporate ladder. Taker tactics of intimidation are directed at rivals on a regular basis. It's an all-important fact of life. Sexual harassment is a form of bullying that Takers invented in order to exert their power over Givers. (Yes, women harass men sexually, too.)

Does your mate sometimes have to tiptoe around you? If this segment pushes your buttons, check the box above.

❐ Givers are less intimidating.

Certainly, some Givers are bullies. But when the tallies are taken, Giver intimidators are outnumbered by Takers. Why? Because Givers get less intimacy by threatening others. Giver traits such as being apologetic, empathetic, indirect, indecisive, and approval-seeking are non-threatening; they exist to forge bonds, not shatter them. Givers would rather relate to others than make them cower.

Are you incapable of intimidating others? Do you sometimes fear your mate? Have you been called a "wuss" ? If this section hints at you, mark the box above.

15. JEALOUSY

☐ Takers are flirty.

The average Taker is unaware of his flirting behavior and seductive powers. It is the Giver who usually points this out to his/her mate after an incident at a cocktail party. "What do you mean I was flirting with Josh?" the seemingly baffled Taker remarks. "We were just having a friendly chat about solar power. I wasn't being coquettish!"

Takers are hardly ever jealous of their mates. They do not need to be. Their Giver lover is so loyal and doting that they cannot imagine infidelity. But when a male Taker is jealous, watch out! He becomes enraged and controlling—and may lock his partner in the house.

Who has gotten into the most trouble for flirting in your relationships? If it's you, check the box above.

☐ Givers get jealous easily.

Givers are continually plagued by this painful emotion. Some take pride in repressing their jealousy—being cool. They express their pain rarely because they fear losing their mate if they are too overt.

Givers have good reason to be jealous of the majority of Takers. Besides being natural-born flirts, the Takers (unbeknownst even to themselves) get off on seeing a Giver in a jealous rage. To them, it is a display of love and servitude. Givers, on the other hand, do not enjoy hurting a mate by creating love triangles. It hurts a Giver too much to hurt someone else.

In most relationships, there is just one truly jealous person. It is usually the Giver. If you turn green more than your mate, check the box.

16. LOVE ADDICTION

☐ Takers want to be adored.

Takers worship their lovers less frequently than Givers do. Their stronger sense of self doesn't allow them to be consumed by another person. If they do become infatuated, they get over it quickly.

Actor Cary Grant was worshipped by his Giver wife Dyan Cannon who, after she divorced him, said, "I had been with Cary four years and really loved him—which means I adored him, I revered him, he was like a God. But none of those things a happy marriage make."

Are you the partner "put on a pedestal" ? If yes, check the box above.

☐ Givers like to worship others.

Everyone wants to love and be loved. But Givers more easily lose themselves in love, becoming overly dependent and needy, suffering pain when a lover is unavailable, emotionally or physically, literally feeling that "I can't live without him."

In Love and Addiction, Dr. Stanton Peele writes: "Love-addiction is discontinued when a person possesses a tangible sense of freedom and self-command—a sense of having power to fashion the conditions of his or her life instead of being fashioned by them."

In your romantic relationships, are you the one who adores his or her partner—and has a compulsive need to be together. If so, check the box.

17. MARRIAGE

☐ Takers are commitmentphobes.

Takers, more than Givers, find themselves in ambivalent relationships. They don't want to marry or dump their mate, so when the subject of marriage comes up, they change it abruptly, talk about it cynically, or agree to talk about it later—"after I've become the CEO of the company or can afford a Ferrari."

Some Takers encourage Givers to fantasize: "After we get married, we'll buy a ski chalet..." This tactic tricks Givers into thinking they have a commitment when, in fact, they do not.

Why do Takers balk? One Taker told us, "If Jenny and I spend more time together, I'll feel smothered. Too much interaction drains me." Takers need to control distance with others, so they will not feel engulfed, and marriage with its daily domestic component threatens distance. If this describes you, check the box.

☐ Givers need a commitment.

A relationship in which one party wants a commitment and the other doesn't is unequal—the uncommitted person is one-up and the committed person is one-down. More Givers find themselves one-down in unequal partnerships.

Even though a Giver may fear commitment, they have many other fears, needs, and instincts that urge them to bond with a mate. Relationships are their lifeblood.

Have you desperately wanted your mate to commit to your future together and then been put on hold? If so, check the box above.

18. MONEY

☐ Takers keep more for themselves.

Most people covet money, but there is a difference between how the Taker and the Giver handle it—the Taker keeps more of his for himself. As a spouse, the Taker gets control of the money and doles it out to the Giver who complains that he is "tight" or a "cheapskate."

Some penniless, youthful Takers arrange to be taken care of by affluent older Givers/Takers who find them sexy. Trophy wives and husbands fall into this category.

Some Takers act overly-generous to get things. Beware.

Are you tight-fisted with your money and dislike sharing it with others? If so, check the box above.

☐ Givers give more to others.

Givers use money to communicate their undying love and devotion. They frequently, and for no particular reason, buy their mates presents: shirts, flowers, jewelry, funny cards, special evenings. They are always thinking of little niceties to surprise their mate.

Many Givers put their mates through school. Law school, medical school, whatever the need, the Giver is there to fill it. Takers often feel so guilty after being put through school or a business venture that they end up leaving their mates to feel better about themselves. The Giver, in this familiar drama, is left crying in the wings, wondering, "What went wrong? I gave him/her everything. I thought you could win people over by doting on them?"

Do you enjoy buying things for others? If so, check the box above.

19. NAGGING

❒ Takers rarely nag.

Takers can criticize in a swift, biting, petty way, but nagging they rarely do. Nagging is plaintive and annoying. Takers complain is a harsher, more demanding tone—usually in a lower voice.

Givers and Takers are irritated by each other's opposite mannerisms. Givers have other-directed ways—they are overly attentive, nicey-nice, motherly, and jealous. Takers lash out at this stuff. Takers have self-directed ways—they are distant, mercurial, abrupt, and flirtatious. Givers react by nagging; the Taker gets even by retreating.

Are you highly sensitive to nagging? Have you pleaded with your mates to stop? If so, check the box.

❒ Givers frequently nag.

No Giver on this planet will admit to nagging, though most will be accused of it. Givers like to have long talks with Takers about how they have been let down. Perhaps the Taker has been late, inconsiderate, cheap, or emotionally absent. The Taker does not want to hear about it—whatever it is. And why should he/she—the action was intentional, a natural consequence of being self-focused.

Nagging a Taker is fruitless because he/she likes the way he/she is and will not change. At the outset there is a sound of defeat in the whiny Giver's voice. It's like having a person locked to a pillory, pleading for an all-expense-paid trip to Tahiti.

Does your mate accuse you of nagging or being overly critical? And do you deny it? If so, check the box.

20. PLEASING

☐ Takers do as they please.

You've heard the song "I Did It My Way." Well, that's how most Takers do it. Takers are more concerned about attention and respect than pleasing others. Pleasers are approval-seekers and Takers are not.

Takers avoid the pleaser syndrome because, since they are self-focused, they are less afraid to have enemies, to engage in conflict, and to display anger. Also they can deftly say no in such a way that you know they mean it. A Giver's will bends much easier.

Do you do it your way, whenever possible? Is pleasing others a job—not a joy? If so, check the box.

☐ Givers are pleasers.

Givers are so focused on pleasing that they qualify some of their statements with phrases like "I kinda think" and "I sorta feel" and "Are you sure it's all right with you...?" They weaken their stances with hedges and disclaimers.

Because Givers are pleasers, they say no in such a way that you think they don't mean it. Takers wonder, "Why is she so easy, so wishy-washy?" Givers are pleasers because they think it will buy them love, approval, and appreciation.

Actor Joan Collins once said, "Highly sensitive to criticism, I seemed to spend my life trying to do everything to please everybody. Consequently, not only did I not please myself, but I was so busy being what others wanted me to be that I almost assumed another identity." If you're a pleaser like Joan, check the box above.

21. POLYGAMY

☐ Takers can be polygamous.

Polygamy is a natural outcome of self-absorption. If attention is predominantly on oneself, then the outer world is merely a candy store full of goodies. Polygamous Takers have mistresses, stealthy lunch dates, get phone calls from admirers, and flirt in front of their mates. The married man or woman who goes out on this spouse is usually a polygamous Taker—and the other woman/man is a Giver who behaves much like the spouse.

Some Takers experience pride for remaining faithful because, for them, infidelity requires a special effort.. Also, they may constantly remind their mates of their self-sacrificing allegiance, pointing out what admirable people they are to decline adultery.

Do you find yourself craving more than one person?

☐ Givers are usually monogamous.

Givers become emotionally involved with one person and stick to them like glue. Don Juan or Juanita could walk by and the Giver would only have eyes for his/her lover. How could a Giver be snowed by more than one person? All of his energy is being used up over one love—there is no energy left. The word "infatuated" was invented for describing Givers.

Certainly, Givers must occasionally think of someone else. Maybe there are problems in their relationship. Maybe they have been together a long time and boredom is setting in. Givers can stray, but compared to Takers, it is a rare event. Does this describe you?

22. POSTURE

❑ Takers lean backwards.

Taking is a pulling action which causes the body to lean backwards. When you observe couples sitting at dinner in a restaurant, notice how the Taker is either upright or reclining backwards. A Taker's arms are less often on the table while talking. Of course, Takers do sit forward, but not as frequently or as far as Givers do.

As a couple is ambling down the street, the Taker is the one who is looking forward and standing more erect. The Taker's walk is more confident, often giving the impression that he is oblivious to the Giver walking beside him. Who in your relationship usually has the more aloof, leaning-backward stance? If its you, mark the box.

❑ Givers lean forward.

Giving is a pushing action which causes the body to lean forward. The person spending more time leaning forward in a dinner conversation is almost always the Giver. The Giver talks more, and the forward position enables him to be heard. The Giver rarely sits back in his seat.

As a couple strolls down the street, the Giver often turns toward the Taker. The Giver's shoulders are often hunched over and bending toward his/her mate. This posture is clingy and overly attentive. In both instances, the Giver's outer-directness causes him/her to lean toward others.

Are you the forward-leaning partner in your relationships? If so, mark the box above.

23. PROJECTING

❐ Takers think everyone is a Taker.

"Everyone's out to get me!" That's what a die-hard Taker thinks. "Gotta watch my backside." A Taker can be dating, or working beside, a die-soft Giver and worry about getting ripped-off. Heavy Takers cannot believe that Givers really are that nice—and not out to get them.

Because Takers project their own behavior onto others, they see a world full of Takers. For instance, Jezabel seldom answers the phone until she hears the caller's voice on her answering machine. She thinks people want to steal her time. "They're constantly asking me do things. Don't they realize I have to....." The word "inconvenienced" pops out of her mouth frequently.

Do you see a world full of grasping Takers? If so, you may be one. Check the box here.

❐ Givers think everyone is a Giver.

To Givers, everyone is an Giver—or a Giver who is not being herself or himself. Takers don't exist. Flaming con-artists are simply Givers in need of love. When Givers are betrayed, they are shocked, dumfounded. "I can't believe she did that, can you?" Or, "What if she never pays me back?"

Givers constantly kvetch about rude behavior. But when it comes to stopping it, they recoil. They get stuck in shock and disbelief. Projecting Giver behavior onto others makes it difficult for Givers to see the truth—that some people really are heavy Takers.

Do you tend to always see the best in the worst people? Have you been called naive and gullible when it come to judging others? If so, check the box.

24. SADISM-MASOCHISM

☐ Takers can be sadistic.

Many Takers unconsciously perform acts to hurt their mates. The Givers become defensive and afraid, and then the Takers feel powerful, elated, and guilty. The cruel Taker is the master and the Giver is the victim or slave. The Taker hurts the Giver by being cold, flirting, by belittling, and by betraying trust.

Why does the Taker want to hurt the Giver? The Taker in actuality striking at himself—but the blow is directed outward. Takers hate themselves for not making much of a contribution to anyone except themselves. Taking more from your mate than you give is a form of cruelty. Have you been called cruel by your mate? If so, check the box.

☐ Givers can be masochistic.

Many Givers unconsciously enjoy being hurt by their Taker mates. "Feeling hurt" turns Givers on because they like being emotional—a connection to the outer world and the Taker who is this world to them. Being emotional is the closest they come to having an inner life of their own. Takers, on the other hand, "feel" constantly, without any need for provocation from the outer world.

Besides using being hurt as an opportunity to feel energized, Givers use it to beg for love. Givers, being unable to receive love that comes too easily, feel that they have to plead, beg, and urge their mates to love them. And how can you behave pleadingly unless someone is doing the opposite—hurting you?

Have you ever been called masochistic or a victim? If so, check the box above.

25. SEX APPEAL

☐ A Taker's sex appeal is cooler.

"Who is that mystery man/woman?" Takers, more than Givers, are alluring, charming, and seductive. They have a way about them that hypnotizes Givers. How do they do it? Givers try to emulate them and fall short.

Takers are sexier because they are more inner-directed; their consciousness is on themselves as they walk, talk, and laugh. (Givers are thinking of others, and this, paradoxically has a negative affect on their appeal.)

Takers have other qualities that add to their allure. They have fewer facial expressions than Givers Many look like a hearty laugh would cause their face to crack. Takers also dress the part. More Taker women wear clingy pants and skimpy dresses—and have long red fingernails. Are you mysteriously seductive? If so, check the box above.

☐ A Giver's sex appeal is warmer.

Givers don't have that magical "t" that Takers possess. This news will be unpleasant to Givers brave enough to accept the fact. Granted, some Givers have more allure than others, but as a group they comes across as too friendly, too nice, to be seductive.

Givers don't have the "fashion model walk." As they charge down the street, their attention is less on their bodies and more on the outer world. Consequently, they walk less erect, less swaggering, and more loosely. Many Giver women's clothing lacks accessories, and far too many wear their blouses outside their slacks to hide their tummies. Do the comments in this section describe you? If so, check the box above.

26. SUPPORTIVENESS

❐ Takers are less supportive.

Takers unconsciously attract a tremendous amount of Giver energy. Oftentimes, a Taker doesn't want help and a multitude of Givers will swarm around him. What can he do? In addition to being mysteriously attractive, the Taker gets supported because he is not too proud to ask. The Takers who demand obnoxiously don't get as much as the charmers—the biggest energy drainers of all.

Takers can be supportive, but they give with a return in mind and they monitor the amount of energy they expend. Takers get a lot of mileage out of what support they give. They make a big fuss over their munificence. Does this hit home? If so, check the box.

❐ Givers are more supportive.

Givers feel closest to their outer world when they are giving to someone. They love to help their friends and lovers. Givers say things like, "I'll get it for you," and "Is there anything you need?"

On the other hand, Givers often decline help for themselves. "That's okay, I can do it myself." Because Givers feel more comfortable giving and less comfortable receiving, they are the perfect mates for Takers.

Givers support Takers through school and encourage them in business. Some Givers even go to school to learn about what their mate needs to know, so they can be of greater support. No mate is totally unsupportive, and Takers give at least 10 percent. The uncalculating Giver thinks it's more. Did we describe you?

27. TEMPERAMENT

☐ Takers tend to be hot-and-cold.

Takers can be warm and friendly one minute, cold and distant the next. You don't know what to expect. Don't blame them. Their demanding inner world is buffeting them around. (It is a wise Taker who is aware of his Jekyll-and-Hyde tendencies and gains control.)

"When she was good/She was very, very good,/ But when she was bad, /She was horrid." That describes Takers to a tee—the men and the women. Givers feel intimidated by Taker unpredictability, but they should not take it personally—as acceptance or rejection. In fact, ironically, one of the reasons Givers are so sexually attracted to Takers is because they cannot figure them out.

Of course, some Takers are mellow and have a mask over their split personality. These Takers are easier to live with. If you are described above, check the box.

☐ Givers are more even-tempered.

Givers are said to be "the same all of the time"—except when they are mad at Takers. They tend to be cheerful and easygoing, bringing stability to their arena. Why? Because their inner world is less tumultuous. Takers get mad because of inner turmoil, while Givers get mad because of the behavior of other people.

Givers are cheerful most of the time because they are giving is some way almost constantly. Giving makes a person feel good. Givers can be spotted by their broad animated smiles, whereas Takers' faces are immobile except when they are in the act of charming someone.

Do you tend to be less moody than your mates?

28. TRUSTING

❐ Takers are less trustworthy.

Takers can be totally trustworthy, totally unreliable, or somewhere in between—what we call trustworthy-at-my-convenience. Takers who are dependable realize that in the long run you get more by keeping your word than by breaking agreements. Unfortunately, the majority of Takers will take the shirt off your back if you are not looking. So you will find a great range of behavior in the trust department, whereas almost all Givers can be trusted above and beyond the call of duty.

Many Takers are reliable at work and untrustworthy at home. Their mates let them get by with being dishonest and unreliable. When an incident occurs, the Giver is quick to forgive. This encourages the Taker to repeat the offense. Ring a bell?

❐ Givers are more trustworthy.

Givers feel dreadful if they break an appointment with a friend. They can be terribly apologetic. "Oh, I'm sorry; did I mess up your schedule?" Keeping agreements is a way of demonstrating how much you value other people.

Takers trust their Giver mates to be honest, not to cheat on them, to remember birthdays and anniversaries, to pay debts on time, and to be consistently attentive. A Taker is correct to trust Givers. Because Givers are so trustworthy, they expect it of others, and are upset when their mates let them down. And since they are attracted to Takers, this is inevitable. Does this describe your situation?

29. WEIGHT

❏ Fewer Takers have weight problems.

Everyone wants to be thin, but Takers, in general, have fewer weight problems. That's because Takers are more in touch with their bodies than Givers. We keep repeating that Takers are more aware of their bodies, and the proof is seen in professional models, the quintessential Takers.

Because Takers are significantly more aware of their bodies, they feel their food to a greater degree while eating. And they usually eat more slowly, a proven factor in weight reduction and maintenance. Are you the slim one?

❏ More Givers have weight problems.

If you see a couple walking down the street and one partner is pudgy, it usually the Giver. Givers are born trenchermen! It is usually they who "wolf it down" after they have just put down a diet book. We know that 50 percent of Americans are overweight, and the greatest percentage of these people are Givers. Since Givers expend much more energy than they receive, there is bound to be an energy drain. Giver then eat to make up the loss. Being more emotional and anxious creates a demand for more food.

Then, too, Givers are not as concerned with their physical appearance as Takers are. Givers think about their looks occasionally, where Takers are obsessed (unconsciously perhaps) with theirs.

Who is flabbier, you or your mate? Who's weight goes up and down like a yo-yo? And who eats the whole carton of ice cream—or dreams about it?

30. WORK

❏ Takers are less service-oriented.

Both Givers and Takers fill every job description, and in many occupations, one type dominates. In sales Takers thrive, mainly because they are better than Givers at coping with rejection—and Taker charm is a great sales tool.

Many Takers are doctors, dentists, and lawyers. These appear to be service jobs, but since the professions offer an abundance of power and money, the Taker is drawn to them. The glamour jobs attract Takers, too—modeling, acting, and professional sports.

Takers can be very quiet and alone, so jobs that require little public contact appeal to them—writing, accounting, lab work, and engineering. We have not done a study on careers, but it is usually obvious who the more dominant type is in each profession.

❏ Givers are more service-oriented.

Almost all nurses are Givers. So are clerks, teachers, dental hygienists, waiters and waitresses. For a Taker to be a waitress, the job would have to deliver excellent tips and require a seductive smile. A Giver woman could be seen at Denny's in a pink uniform collecting sixty-five-cent gratuities.

Are you starting to get the hang of it? We will not be able to discuss many jobs on one page, but if the job requires sympathy, nurturing, or support, than it usually attracts Givers. How many nurses do you know who are glamorous Taker types? Most are plain, hefty Givers. What Taker is going to want to change bedpans and bathe strangers?

Now Record Your Responses...

Are you starting to get a sense of the energy the over-generous Giver expends in day-to-day life situations? The Taker loses less energy, conserving it for himself or herself.

The next page is a tally sheet for the traits you have just read. By using this sheet you will be able to see whether your energy is primarily going to others or to yourself—whether you are a more of a Giver or a Taker.

Turn back to the subjects in this chapter and then mark corresponding boxes on this page. You answered Giver and Taker, and your answers will fall in both columns. No one has gotten all of their answers only on one side or the other.

The column with the most answers tells you whether you are a Giver or Taker. The column with the least answers tells you which reality you need to develop in order to become a more Balanced person.

The Giver-Taker Tally Sheet

Taker Box Checked: **Giver Box Checked:**

_____   **Apologies**   _____

_____   **Breaking Up**   _____

_____   **Changing People**   _____

_____   **Communication**   _____

_____   **Conflict**   _____

_____   **Control**   _____

_____   **Decisiveness**   _____

_____   **Engulfment**   _____

_____   **Expectations**   _____

_____   **Face Value**   _____

_____   **Feelings**   _____

_____   **Friendships**   _____

_____   **Giving Orders**   _____

_____   **Intimidation**   _____

_____	**Jealousy**	_____
_____	**Love Addiction**	_____
_____	**Marriage**	_____
_____	**Money**	_____
_____	**Nagging**	_____
_____	**Pleasing Others**	_____
_____	**Polygamy**	_____
_____	**Posture**	_____
_____	**Projecting**	_____
_____	**Sadism-Masochism**	_____
_____	**Sex Appeal**	_____
_____	**Supportiveness**	_____
_____	**Temperament**	_____
_____	**Trusting**	_____
_____	**Weight Problems**	_____
_____	**Work**	_____

**Record the number of answers on each side.
Find out if you are *primarily* a Giver or a Taker.**

Your Totals:

✎_____   ✎_____

Are you more of a Giver or more of a Taker? "Primarily" means you do it more than fifty-percent of the time. No one has gotten all of their answers only on one side or the other. Most of us are unbalanced to some degree. If you got a perfect score in one column, you win the first whack at the pinata.

The Tally Sheet is a crude assessment because it covers only thirty traits and asks for just one response for each one. Consequently, a Heavy Giver and a Light Giver, or a Heavy Taker and Light Taker, could have similar totals. Your score is a guesstimate.

Our friend, Melissa, said, "For some of the traits, I couldn't decide which one I was." Her response is common. Just do your best and don't worry if you were unable to come to a clear decision for each trait.

Again, the column with the most answers tells you whether you are more of a Giver or Taker. The column with the least answers tells you which reality you need to develop in order to become more Balanced.

-3-

Who Chases Whom?

It's an old game.
One person chases the other,
and it goes back and forth,
the Giver in pursuit of the Taker,
most of the time.

Takers are chased more than Givers. They are pursued by Givers, though they never really get caught, appearances to the contrary. Takers love being sought after. It gives them a sense of command.

Takers can outrun Givers easily, and when it looks as if the Giver is getting weary, they stop and wait for the poor creature to regain energy. At this point, even the adoring Giver may stop chasing. This worries the Taker, who will actually chase the Giver if it appears the Giver is backing off. Thus, there appears to be a kind of back-and-forth dance between Giver and Taker lovers.

How do Takers keep Givers guessing? One way is to space their phone calls to suit their own convenience. Givers are never sure when the blessed call will come and are kept in a constant state of anticipation. Another Taker tactic in running from a Giver is to withdraw attention and communication without reason. Nothing is more prone to drive a Giver into a frenzy!

The Taker, in general, wants to keep the outer world, which makes him feel uncomfortable, at a distance. Many Takers actually fear closeness.

Takers view their lovers as clingy, possessive, demanding, and weak. Takers do not respect Givers for chasing them, yet if they are not being chased they feel uneasy. It is a losing game. For Takers both love and hate being chased by Givers suitors.

Now let's look at the game from the Giver point of view: When Givers are with a person of the opposite sex who is very nice to them they get bored. Parents of Givers say things like, "Why don't you date Jeremy? He's so nice to you." The Giver replies plaintively, "Yes, but he's boring." Simultaneously Givers reprimand themselves with, "Why can't I like Jeremy? He does so many thoughtful things for me...but he doesn't turn me on." It is a real problem for most Givers, silly as it sounds: the lure of the inaccessible person.

Givers not only like to chase—they must do the chasing or else they are not interested. Synonyms for "chase," in this context, are "idolize," "worship," and "adore." Givers think their lovers are "really cute" or "very handsome" or "stunningly beautiful." The Giver falls into this trap because he is outer-directed. Others have a greater reality for him, hence a greater beauty.

Givers might be cured of their illusions if they know how uninterested Takers are in them. The Giver will never be adored if he dates Takers. Takers are inner-directed and only worship themselves. So what one finds in many relationships is an adorer and an adored. One-sided love is the norm.

One person chases the other, and it goes back and forth, the Giver in pursuit of the Taker most of the time. It's an old game, and it is unpleasant, especially for the Givers.

Lori and Trevor

Infuriated by Trevor's Taker ways, Lori frequently stormed out of their condo sobbing. (Ironically, Trevor fell for Lori because of her fiery spirit.) Their relationship began to unravel as marriage-minded Lori became insecure about losing her hunky guy and turned suffocating, possessive, and jealous.

"She's smothering me," Trevor told pals. "She complains if I'm away too long, if I drink too much, and if I want to hang out with my buddies. She goes crazy when I don't call her several times a day."

Hoping to please her 36-year-old beau, Lori, 38, reversed her decision not to have more children, and decided to undergo plastic surgery to look sexier for Trevor whose previous girlfriend was in her mid-twenties.

During the Christmas holidays, Lori visited her brother in Vermont but couldn't get her mind off Trevor. She had hoped they would spend New Year's Eve together, but he would have no part of it. Instead, he gave a big party in London for his former rock band. Tormented, Lori did everything in her power to put Trevor out of her mind. Nothing worked so she called him several times a day. He ducked her calls.

After three years of a back-and-forth romance, Lori and Trevor split up, leaving her heartbroken and in tears. A year later, Lori still pines for Trevor, replaying their final kiss over and over again in her mind. "He aroused me so completely. I was so hot for him." Meanwhile, Trevor is being chased by Victoria, a 40-year-old woman who is considering liposuction.

When we last talked with Lori, she said, "I see myself as being articulate and forceful in a work environment, telling my boss and co-workers exactly what I think. I'm strong at work but not in my love life. I'm really aware of the discrepancy."

Trevor has few complaints. Sure, he feels smothered by fawning women, but that's the price he pays for being adored—and for him adoration is the only form of love he understands. In Trevor's love relationships, he is the master of his-and-her universe.

High-Flying Adored

Nancy Milford's biography, *Savage Beauty*, explores the life of Edna St. Vincent Millay, the first woman to win the Pulitzer Prize for verse. What follows are some of Milford's quotes and opinions about Edna, a consummate Taker:

"One cannot really write about Edna Millay without bringing into the foreground of the picture her intoxicating effect on people."

"She was one of those women...who, excited by blood or the spirit, became almost supernaturally beautiful." Edna's bobbed-hair was the color of fire, thick and curly. Her skin was as pale as milk.

"She was a little bitch, a genius, a cross between a gamin and an angel....She really never loved anyone except herself."

"While her heart is still in the grave of one love affair, she is making eyes at another man."

John Peale Bishop and Edmund Wilson, close friends and editors at *Vanity Fair*, fell in love with Edna. She complained that their both being in love with her hadn't even broken up their friendship.

Wilson once told her, "Your many admirers should form an alumni association." She answered promptly, "We always talk about it, but we never do it."

Edna was gutsy. Once she told a Giver woman friend, "When a man looks at you, you simply look back. Or ask him for something, for a match." The Giver replied, "Edna, men don't ask me for a match, or for the time. And if I'm going to the post office for a stamp, I come home with one. I don't meet a man."

The public was enchanted with Millay. "Tickets for her poetry readings were wildly sought-after whether she was in Oklahoma or Chicago, where the hall seating 1,600 was sold out and even with standees they had to take an extra hall for the overflow of another 800 who listened to her over amplifiers."

Author Thomas Hardy once said, "There are really only two great things in the United States, the skyscraper and the poetry of Edna St. Vincent Millay."

-4-

The Taker's Secret Code

The Taker, unbeknownst to himself or herself,
has a code of reciprocating,
a set way of giving that is peculiar
to the individual.

People who are very beautiful
make their own laws."

—*VIVIEN LEIGH*
The Roman Spring of Mrs. Stone

"He's the only person I know who
can strut sitting down."

—*GENE KELLY*
in Inherit the Wind

Takers do give, but they do it differently than Givers. They do it, as we have explained before, based on a strong focus on the self. They suffer from a distance between themselves and the outside world. It is difficult to give to something that seems so far away, so alien. Below is a simple description of the different ways in which the two types give.

Takers give more reluctantly, sporadically, and always for a calculated reason. Givers give more automatically, constantly, and always for another's love, approval, and appreciation.

Takers think before they give, and because they act reluctant. Givers often do not press them to do so. Givers, on the other hand, are like automatons, performing kindnesses without conscious intention to do so. Givers constantly bestow and occasionally get burned in their constant quest for approval from others. Takers do not expend their energy seeking approval from others. When they do give, they give for a specific reason.

7 Reasons Why Takers Give

(1) Takers sometimes give to make relationships appear equal. They intuitively know that others are watching them.

(2) Takers give to feel less guilty. Takers unconsciously feel guilty for receiving more than they give. Their guilt is lessened by token acts of giving.

(3) Takers give to win confrontations. People often accuse Takers of being unfair, so they give a little when it really counts.

(4) Takers give with a token gesture after a blatant act of taking. When a Taker gets a windfall of goodies, he/she reciprocates immediately in a tokenistic way to appear grateful. For example, a Taker plumber gives flowers to the sick wife of a contractor who has just hired him for a $5,000 job.

(5) Takers give to have a respectable public image.

Takers are success oriented and want to be well thought of, so they give, usually in an overt way, every now and then,

(6) Takers actually enjoy giving on occasion. Takers are not totally coldhearted. They get some pleasure in seeing another's joy as a result of their benevolence. It does not, however, change the trend of their lives, which is to take at least ten times what they must give.

(7) Takers are taught good manners by parents, teachers, and society. They realize that courtesy and kindness, even faked, pay dividends—like T-bills and money market certificates.

～ ～ ～

We know that Givers who have just read the list above are saying to themselves, "I do all of those things, too." Yes, you do, but not nearly as often. The above behavior is much more frequently found among Takers than Givers. Why? Because Givers are less calculating and think less before acting. Givers have a hard time adding up what they have given and what they have received. Takers are geniuses when it comes to calculating the energy they have expended. Givers need to take Smart Pills—or smart from overindulging users.

The Code of Reciprocation

A code is a system of rules. The Taker, unbeknownst to himself or herself, has a code of reciprocating, a set way of giving that is peculiar to the individual. Each Taker's code provides for a finite number of situations in which that Taker will give, no less and no more.

The Giver has no such code. The Giver gives to selected individuals, but there is no limit to what the Giver will do for those targets of affection. The Giver is flexible in his giving, much of it is unpredictable.

When you meet a Taker it is wise to determine his/her Code of Reciprocation. Some Takers, for instance, will rush into a burning building to save a child's life, some will not. Some Takers will never betray their friends; others will do so readily.

Brent

Meet Brent. He is a Taker and he gives by remembering birthdays of those closest to him. On his wife Jennifer's birthday, for instance, he buys her a dozen roses and takes her to dinner. Every year he does the same thing. He also is affectionate most of the time. He always asks his wife what movie she wants to see whenever they go to a movie. He is considerate in many ways, many predictable ways. Jennifer is not big on birthdays, but she keeps his house, raises his two children, feeds him well, helps him buy his wardrobe (three times the size of hers), and holds down a job. Brent's friends think he is one helluva a guy. Jenny loves him, but knows he is a Taker.

Heather

She is Taker who gives in many clever ways. She helps her women friends whenever they move into a new apartment. She lines their shelves. Even more useful is the fact that she has boyfriends handy to rent and drive a truck for the occasion. When Heather has people to dinner, they are treated to gourmet cooking. If someone she knows is ill, she quickly reacts with hot pads and chicken soup, organic orange juice and good advice. She does these and other acts of giving. But as a whole, the world revolves around Heather. She is a "barracuda," even though she is capable of the occasional giving gesture.

The only time she lent money to a friend she demanded nine-percent interest, and kept some jewelry as collateral. She never telephones her parents because they live in another state and she does not like to pay for long distance phone calls, even though she is financially better off than they are. Heather has made clear, firm decisions about when she will give—and when she will not, and the later occasions far outnumber the former.

Takers Can Be Mistaken for Givers

It is a clever person who can consistently distinguish Takers from Givers. The Code of Reciprocation is the mask Takers use to hide their overall intentions. Takers give in a calculating, sporadic way that resembles a Giver's style if one is unaware of the Taker's long-term pattern of giving only in fits and starts. Takers can adapt the same sweet smile and use the same cliches so natural to Givers. Givers invent an appropriate language for giving and Takers borrow it from them.

It Takes One to Know One

Takers have trouble taking from each other. They understand each other too well. The only person a Taker can conquer is an unsuspecting, gullible Giver. Takers often watch other Takers in action, and at the same time, make mental notes on tricks they themselves might wish to use in the future. In addition, the acts that make up one Taker's Code of Reciprocation do not fool another Taker into thinking he is with a Giver.

We have heard accounts of Takers who help their Giver mate deal with other Takers in business. Takers know their spouse or mate is naive, and they want to protect them against other Takers. The wise Giver will trust a Taker in this instance, and heed good advice.

-5-

The Lovers' Triangle

*In the course of a lifetime,
most people are victims of a least one
Lovers' Triangle.*

"The best case against going with a married man is not the futility of it—it's finally getting him. Then what do you have? A husband who cheats on his wife. Some bargain."

—ABIGAIL VAN BUREN

The Lover's Triangle almost always consists of two Givers and one Taker. The two Givers both want the attractive Taker, and the Taker—no matter how he may protest—secretly wants the attention of two people. Two suitors is always more flattering than one, to the Taker's way of thinking. Giver 1 despises Giver 2 and plots to retain the full control of the Taker. Giver 2 wants to get the original Giver out of the picture as soon as possible, but feels guilty for inflicting pain on another.

The Taker, of course, relishes being the center of attention, not to mention being in the driver's seat. Takers are polygamous by nature; Givers are monogamous.

So the Taker is pleased to be chase by his Givers. Eventually, because of the hatred of the two Givers for each other, the Taker is forced to choose between them, opting for the new mate or the old one. It is a difficult choice and causes the Taker to fret because he wants his cake and wants to eat it, too. If one Giver is wealthier than the other, the decision is easier. Takers migrate to economic rewards.

The Two Givers Won't
Dump the Taker

In a situation where both Givers know about each another, and both love the Taker passionately, rarely does either Giver take the simple course of action, leaving, which would end her misery. The Givers are so pitted against each other and so blinded by Taker charm that giving him up is impossible.

Givers know it would be wise to let go of the Taker, but cannot act upon their good common sense. Givers are too emotional, and their emotions rule their actions. The Takers know this and take full advantage of the fact. He would be surprised if he were turned out.

The ballsy Taker feels secure as the man in charge, the officer in command, the dominant partner in his love triangle. The astute observer has noted that the Taker is polygamous and sadistic while the Givers are being monogamous and masochistic. A Balanced person, needless to say, would extricate herself from such a melodrama at the first opportunity.

Businessman, Dutiful Wife, and Sexy Mistress

The Taker executive can often keep this variation of the Lovers' Triangle going for years. He tells his mistress that his wife is unbearable, but he can't leave her because she will sue him for all he has.

Since the Taker loves himself and his money more than either woman, he both uses and assuages both women. He talks to his mistress about how harpy, boring, and wrinkled his wife is, and is clever enough never to discuss the mistress with his wife. She is kept in the dark, although she suspects her Taker husband is philandering. These situations have an element of farce, but they are also filled with intrigue, deceit, and pain. The two Givers will suffer the most. They maybe dropped at any moment, while the Taker is always in control.

☞　☞　☞

In this triangle, the mistress is usually a Giver, but sometimes she can also be a Taker. If a Giver, like the woman above, she desperately wants to marry the businessman and loves him despite his bald pate and sun-parched face. But if he is hairy and handsome, for his age, she becomes hopelessly smitten. Remember, Givers need to adore their significant others. By contrast, Taker women caught in a triangle care more about their Nordstrom's clothing allowance and luxury apartment, paid for by an affluent Taker who can be replaced.

Another difference: The Giver mistress siphons off some of her lover's money and send it to friends and relatives, while the Taker mistress mails some of hers to a bank account in the Bahamas.

Was Marla Trump a Giver or a Taker mistress? What about Camilla? And Cleopatra? (Her appeal, strength, and command—and dominance of Antony—was legend.) In a future edition, we plan to expand this section to include several titilating stories about famous mistresses' and their Giver/Taker ways of being.

-6-

Rating
the
Two
Types

Givers are looking for someone to give to;
Takers are looking for someone to take from.
Givers and Takers mate with each other
by necessity.   Opposites attract.

"Adoring someone is certainly better than being adored.
Being adored is a nuisance. You'll discover, Dorian,
that women treat us just as humanity treats its gods.
They worship us but keep bothering us to
do something for them."

—GEORGE SANDERS
The Picture of Dorian Gray

When you analyze people's behavior, ask, "To what degree is he/she more of a Giver or more of a Taker?" Nevermind that on Monday she was very, very nice and on Tuesday she was very, very rotten. Try to see the big picture—the overall trend. Toss out your magnifying glass.

It is not enough to know whether your mate and the people you deal with are Givers or Takers. You must estimate the degree which the role is played. Your estimate will help you predict another's future reactions, and it will help you know how much to give or receive in your dealings with people. Below we rate the two types.

Extremes— *Tens*

On a tenscale, these people are the tens. These Givers and Takers hurt themselves, others, or both excessively in a variety of ways. This category includes people with complicated psychological problems such as battered wives, criminals, rapists, suicidals, addicts, etc. Elvis Presley, Judy Garland, John Belushi, Adolf Hitler, Marilyn Monroe, and Zelda Fitzgerald are but a few examples.

The tragic problem of the battered woman comes readily to mind when we talk about extremes. This woman (a Giver) allows her body to be beaten and then afterwards consoles her repentant husband (a Taker). In her book *The Battered Woman*, Lenore E Walker describes men who batter. "The women interviewed all described their batterers as having a dual personality, much like Dr. Jekyll and Mr. Hyde. The batterer can either be very, very good, or very, very horrid. Furthermore, he can swing back and forth between the two characters with the smoothness of a con artist. Most batterers feel a sense of guilt and shame at his uncontrollable actions. If he were able to cease the violence he would." Ms. Walker in her description has, in our opinion, given an accurate description of an Extreme Taker.

The battered woman is in a sense performing a giving act when she allows her husband to take out his frustrations on her body. She provides him with an animated punching bag. Afterwards, when she nurtures or mothers her repentant spouse (or lover), she takes delight in her mate's contriteness, not realizing that her emotional life is dependent upon a destructive relationship she consciously regards as sick.

Heavies—*Sevens, Eights, Nines*

On a tenscale, these people are the sevens, eights, and nines. Their giving-and-taking is obvious, but not extreme. A novice Giver/Taker watcher can easily identify them. We have many names for them:

Hardcore Takers: A brutal and ruthless manipulator. She will use you in any way possible. This person may be mean and unpopular, or obnoxious and quite successful.

Royal Takers: This Taker is into finery—fine cars, homes, jewelry, clothes, and grooming. He usually takes from affluent Givers. Some are referred to as Gold Diggers.

Courteously Attentive Takers: The stealthy CAT gets what he wants by being sweet, polite, and helpful most of the time...and then he does something shocking, like leave you in a puddle of tears at the alter. His subconscious motive: Be nice to Givers and they will help you get ahead.

Resentful Givers: These Givers are bitter, hardened people. Life has been tough for them, and it shows all over their expressive faces. They may look gaunt or puffy from suffering bouts of emotional storms. They're also called martyrs and victims.

Goody-Goodies: No resentment here. These gentle souls like being used and never ask for anything in return. They giggle and grin a lot, and often say, "I'm sorry," even when they are not in anyone's way. Goody-Goodies make doting parents and overly saccharine mates. Pollyanna fits this description.

Moderates—*Fours, Fives, Sixes*

This category is made up of the "average person." The Moderate Givers give far more than mates, think they receive enough, yet sporadically get whiny, resentful, and unpleasant. The Moderate Takers, on the other hand, give far less than their mates, yet think they give plenty. These Takers feel guilty and are unaware of it. Couples made up of Moderates appear to have happy relationships half of the time. People are usually puzzled when they divorce.

Lights—*Ones, Twos, Threes*

These people are the happiest group, and make up less than ten percent of the population. The Light Takers are easily mistaken for Givers, and the Light Givers are prudent about how much and to whom they give. People in this category have a strong sense of self-worth and a kindly manner. Since no one can be perfectly balanced—because of our inborn predisposition to inner- or outer-directness—we can wish at most to emulate the nearly-balanced Lights.

Nice Takers: These Takers give almost as much as they take. They are still Takers because they are born with a dominant subjective reality, and their primary concern is themselves, not others. They are more aware when they give than any Giver is, so there is always an element of self-consciousness in their generosity.

Selective Givers: These Givers do not bestow favors readily to loved ones and others. They are conscious of their own energy, and preserve much of it for themselves. This alone makes them unique among Givers. A Selective Giver woman often chooses to have one or two children, never more. She has a job she enjoys and she will not allow her employers to overwork her. Selective Givers make the effort to look after themselves—an effort all Takers achieve naturally.

Reformed Givers and Takers: These people were at one time the Moderates, Heavies, or Extremes. Somehow they have dimished their own destructive patterns. Through therapy, or life's unkind lessons, these Givers and Takers lowered their numbers on the Giver/Taker Tenscale.

Reformed Givers realize they can be easily used and can backslide inro behavior that is perhaps to self-sacrificing for their own good.

Reformed Takers know that have used others, and have wearied of exploitation.

We hope this book, by creating awareness of how the

two types manipulate and suffer through their own forms of perception, will produce more Reformed Givers and Takers.

Opposites Attract

How do you know if you are a Heavy, Moderate, or Light Giver or Taker? Think about your mate? How would you rate him or her? Consider your partner's overall behavior. Focus on him or her because Opposites Attract—he/she is your mirror image.

Here's how it plays out: Extreme Givers adore Extreme Takers. Heavy Givers worship Heavy Takers. Moderate Givers migrate toward Moderate Takers—and Light Givers select Light Takers.

Have you ever called your mate "extremely self-centered?" If so, then he is an Extreme or a Heavy Taker and you are a Heavy Giver, his opposite. What you have say about your mate is true about you in reverse. Turn your projections around. Likewise, if your mate is nice, considerate, and supportive almost all of the time—and your are, too—then you are one of the lucky few who are in a Light or Balanced relationship.

-7-

The
Remedies

*The Givers of this world do not grasp
the significance of their inner lives, and place
pitifully little value on their own worth.*

*The Takers are determined to bend others
to their will, and in doing so blindly destroy
the very Givers they require to fulfill
their own ambitions.*

Just this once, Kirk, why don't you
empty your own ashtrays.

—EDMUND O'BRIEN
in The Barefoot Contessa

On the following pages, we offer eleven solutions to the Giver/Taker problem. The remedies are common sense notions, easy to remember. Subscribing to any or all of these suggestions will automatically improve your relationships. You will become either a less resentful Giver, or feel less a guilty Taker. You will experience the sensation of having a heavy burden lifted from your life.

The remedies urge you to create balanced relationships. As a Balanced person you will know when to give your time, money, and advice to others—you'll be nobody's fool. And you will know when to receive from people who shower you with gifts.

If the Takers of this world could spend one day as Givers, there would be less warfare. If the Givers could spend one day as Takers, there would be less servility.

REMEDY 1

Give to the Givers,
and take from the Takers.

If you give to Givers, they will protest. Force them to take things. Give them flowers, dinners, back-rubs, and theater tickets. You will be assisting them, helping them develop the ability to receive abundantly. They do receive in some measure, but it is only a fraction of what Takers enjoy.

If you take from Takers, they will protest. Insist that they be fair in all dealings whether they object or not. Be clever, subtle—stay amused. At first you will feel awkward, for you are used to taking from Givers, who readily comply, and are hesitant to ask Takers for anything. Taking from Takers is more challenging, and the victory is sweeter.

REMEDY 2

Don't take too much from Givers,
or give too much to Takers.

It is unwise to take too much from Givers, although they may pressure you to do so. Why? Because Givers have high expectations of how you show gratitude. This may be a burden you are not ready to shoulder. Giving too much to Takers is equally unwise. They lose respect for people who are too easy to dominate. And there is no limit to their greed.

REMEDY 3

If you are a Giver, make an effort
to receive more.

Ask for favors. Expect to be treated well. Do not regard it as a miracle from heaven when people are courteous to you. Try not to talk too much—talking is a way of expending energy.

At first, as a Giver, you will find yourself feeling awkward; you are not used to asking for things. The trick is not to plead or whine. Be straightforward. And don't worry about turning into a Taker yourself. In the first place, Taker charm is inborn. You do not risk becoming a fake Taker, only more nearly balanced.

It is true that you get a lot by being a Taker, but the consequences may be painful. You have to live with and try to cherish a Giver, a resentful gift horse who nags or complains. Is it worth it?

Give abundantly to your Giver mate. Insist on doing half the household chores. Try not to be a parasite—assume your fair share of the financial burdens; or, if you already are sharing costs equally, or are contributing more, try to find more ways of giving to the person you love.

This is the only way to free yourself from the unconscious guilt you feel over letting others do so much for you. You will find yourself propelled by a new energy that will enrich your life.

REMEDY 4
If you are a Taker, make an effort to give more.

It is true that you get a lot by being a Taker, but the consequences may be painful. You have to live with and try to cherish a Giver, a resentful gift horse who nags or complains. Is it worth it?

Give abundantly to your Giver mate. Insist on doing half the household chores. Try not to be a parasite—assume your fair share of the financial burdens; or, if you already are sharing costs equally, or are contributing more, try to find more ways of giving to the person you love.

This is the only way to free yourself from the unconscious guilt you feel over letting others do so much for you. You will find yourself propelled by a new energy that will enrich your life.

REMEDY 5
Become familiar with Taker tricks, designed to get things.

Both Givers and Takers need to become familiar with Taker tricks. This knowledge will help Takers comprehend their own behavior, and it will help Givers learn how they are being used.

Takers simply ask. Takers unabashedly ask others—especially their mates—for favors and emotional support. They do it naturally, smoothly, and continuously. And they are also capable of asking sweetly and harshly in the same hour. Remember, they can be moody.

Takers intimidate.

Most Takers have an inborn talent for inspiring fear in Givers. Their Giver mates will give because they fear the Taker will leave them, be cruel to them, or launch into some form of histrionics. Givers like to concede points. They rush to obey, hoping to calm the water—a temporary diplomatic solution at best.

Takers ask for sympathy.

Takers can handle their own problems, but prefer letting others contribute their energy to the cause. Takers complain a lot. The Givers then responds, "Is there anything I can do to help?" Do not chime in with aid, even though it gives you great pleasure. Once you start giving to a Taker it is hard to stop.

Takers use reverse psychology.

A Taker will tell a Giver he doesn't need something that is the minimum, necessary for comfort. Example: Oh, I don't need a chair; I can sit on the floor..." This clever ploy elicits sympathy and giving.

Takers accuse others of being "selfish."

Of course, Givers throw this accusation at Takers, too. But the Taker just laughs, whereas the Giver usually feels guilty and thinks, "Gee, maybe he's right." Then the Giver comes through with more favors to prove he/she is not selfish. The Taker gloats when this happens.

Takers turn on the charm.

Charm and self-centeredness go together like a latte and a biscotti. Because Givers fall for charm, they find themselves anxious to give to self-absorbed people. Beware of the strikingly appealing lover.

Takers take receiving for granted.

By not constantly acknowledging what they are getting, they keep Givers in the dark as to how much is being done for them.

Takers brag about what they give.

When Takers give, they often praise themselves. "Remember when I took you to dinner last month." And, "Didn't I do a great job of fixing your laptop?" Takers keep a mental record of their good deeds. Givers rarely do; they are too busy giving.

Takers fake incompetence.

Just tell a Giver she/he can do a job better and see what happens. Takers know that Givers are flattered by this tactic.

Givers are outer-directed and require approval from others, and thus are easy marks for flattery.

Takers say, "I'll do it," and then don't.

Many a Taker has conserved his/her energy by agreeing to do something and then calmly and with no apparent malice breaking the agreement. They shrug off their Givers' anxiety and then charm them. A Taker may explain his/her misdemeanor with, "I was too busy with more important things," even if he was just watching a football game or she was just returning a dress.

Takers ignore requests.

Takers also use the silent treatment to get out of doing things for others. You may feel as if you are talking to a wall when supplicating a Taker. They know that if you get no response, you will usually walk away perplexed and do the job yourself.

Takers just say "no."

Just as Takers have no trouble asking for things, they have no trouble saying no when they don't want to do something. They are masters of the direct approach. Givers usually feel guilty when they say no.

Takers become testy and irritable.

Asking some Takers to do the smallest favor can be like pulling teeth with rusty pliers. Givers often know in advance they are going to experience heavy resistance and decide not to ask for favors at all. Best to locate the nearest Giver for assistance, or do the job all by yourself.

To understand Takers better, think about how children respond to their parent's requests. If your children are grown, remember what they said when you asked them to clean their room or finish their homework, and they wanted to watch television. Remember "the look" you got. Most kids behave like Takers. It's their job.

REMEDY 6
Become familiar with Giver tricks, designed to avoid receiving.

Givers possess skill at the art of denying themselves. If you are a Giver, you must realize that you believe most of your relationships are reciprocal when they are not. If you are a Taker, read the Giver tricks below and see if your mate uses them. If he/she does, do what you can to get your mate to receive more. Don't let him/her get by with receiving so much less than you do. If you do, you will pay a price. Everything in life must be paid for, in pennies or in blood. Below are the ploys Givers use to avoid receiving. Etch them in your brain.

Givers prefer not to ask.
If they do ask, they preface their request with, "Do you

mind doing me a big favor?" or "If you're too busy, it's not a big deal." Givers shirk from imposing.

Givers can get it themselves.
They are famous for stating, "That's okay; I'll do it by myself." And they follow the words with the deed.

Givers deny themselves.
Givers think that receiving things implies weakness, where-as Takers see aid as adding to their strength. Givers want others to describe them as strong, capable, responsible, and courteous—even when times are tough.

Givers are not as seductive.
Who wants to give to a competent person who does not dress seductively, charm shrewdly, or dominate powerfully? Many Givers are overweight and unappealing. It is much more fun to give to someone with tremendous sex appeal.

Givers are too busy giving.
The sad truth about Givers is that they are so busy giving to others that it literally does not occur to them to ask for phys-ical or emotional support from others—that would take time away from the hectic schedule they have already insist-ed upon establishing for themselves. They are like the grand-mother we know, who invites a dozen people for dinner—and then complains about having to cook for a dozen peo-ple. Or the thirty-five year old man who married a nineteen

year old beauty and had to teach her life skills—how to cook, keep a house, get a job, etc.

Until Givers give themselves the time to receive from others, their lives will persist in an unhealthy and unhappy imbalance. Interestingly, Givers give to a chosen few. They reserve most of their energy for mates, family, friends, and acquaintances. More altruistic Givers can include strangers as recipients, but for the most part, they believe those beyond their small, intimate circle may be ignored. A Giver's generosity has its limits.

REMEDY 7
Be wary of Taker guilt and Giver resentment.

Taker guilt is difficult to spot. If your mate is a Taker, you may be unaware of his/her guilty feelings. How do you spot guilt? If it is not evident to you, you might observe it in the following disguises.

The Taker will attack you for no apparent reason.
The anger, expressed either physically or verbally, that the Taker feels about himself/herself is directed outward. If you are attacked without reason, chances are it is Taker guilt in action.

The Taker will repeat a wrongdoing.

If you condemn a Taker for doing something to you, even something that is blatantly cruel, the Taker will repeat the act to soothe his or her guilt. By repeating the behavior, he is establishing, if only to himself, its correctness. For instance, a Taker who has been unfaithful will cheat on his Giver wife again and again to "prove" that he is right. (Applicable to Givers as well as Takers is the following warning from Sigmund Freud who said, "The compulsion to repeat can be demonic. It can turn against the subject—to the point of self-extinction.")

The Taker often appears melancholy, depressed.

This manifestation of guilt is often misinterpreted by the average Giver, who finds the intermittent moodiness of his Taker mate sexually exciting or even poetic. The Taker's sadness often comes from guilt over not being able to give freely. It is ironic that the Givers of this world are turned on by another's guilt.

Giver resentment is easier to spot than Taker guilt.

Givers tend to wear their hearts on their sleeves while Takers are generally most mysterious. The Giver complains, bitches, nags, or angrily deplores whatever troubles him. Beware of tirades that last for hours, resentments that seem to spring from trivial causes. Givers can go on ad nauseum without apparent reason. Givers supplement present grievances with past complaints.

REMEDY 8

When involved in a Giver/Taker drama, stay amused.

When caught in an encounter with a resentful Giver or a Taker who is projecting his guilt, do your best to stay amused. Both the Giver or Taker will try to provoke you into agreeing with their side of the story in their desperate efforts to escape their own pain. Stay cool. Keep everything light and cheerful. Tactfully show those caught in the Giver/Taker drama how their own attitude is the chief cause of their anguish. Do not let them trick you into thinking that their mates are the sole villains. If they are really making you miserable, show them this page and tell them to take their business to Walmart.

REMEDY 9

Remember that Givers and Takers can always learn from each other.

Your mate—who is your opposite—can teach you about the missing side of your personality. Observe the positive qualities he or she possesses. If you are a Giver, you need to learn how the Taker is more unabashedly able to ask for and receive things. You might admire the way Takers walk, with a poise and an awareness of their bodies those with less impressive posture might study profitably.

Takers need to observe how generous Givers can be. Giver also possess the ability to be more compassionate, a trait absent in many Takers.

REMEDY 10
Bail out when the going gets rough.

It is better to be single than to be in a heavy Giver/Taker drama in which you often cry through the night or are bored beyond all hope.

A very light Giver/Taker drama is tolerable, of course. You are responsible for assessing your own situation and deciding if you are tolerating it out of fear or a misguided pity for your mate.

If you find yourself with an extreme or heavy Giver or Taker, bail out as soon as possible. These people need therapy and you only bring havoc and pain to your life when you choose to tolerate them.

There can be more joy in living alone than living with someone who insists upon playing out the Giver/Taker drama.

REMEDY 11

Strive for balance in
all of your relationships.

Or as Aristotle put it:

"Nothing

in

excess."

To Our Readers

We welcome correspondence concerning this book. Send us your Giver-Taker Story and we may include it—with your written permission, of course—in a future edition.

The Givers & The Takers
P. O. Box 223157
Princeville, HI 96722

HOW TO ORDER BOOKS!

It's easy! Send $12 for each book to the address above. We'll pay for the postage and handling—and we'll mail them to a friend with a gift note and wrapping. For 3-20 books, your cost is less, $10 per book. For over 20, let's talk.